CREATING A SAFE SPACE

IN THE CLASSROOM

A Guide for Educators

Kim Alexander, BA (Hons.), B.Ed, OCT

ISBN 978-1-7779254-0-6 (Paperback)
ISBN 978-1-7779254-2-0 (Hardcover)
ISBN 978-1-7779254-1-3 (eBook)

Edited by Andrea Lemieux
Book production by Dawn James, Publish and Promote
Cover, layout, and interior design by Publish and Promote

Printed and bound in Canada

Disclaimer: The information in this book is for educational purposes only. The author shall have neither liability nor responsibility to any person or entity with respect to any information contained in this book. The reader assumes all risk with respect to any of the information contained in this book, directly or indirectly, by using any information described herein.

CONTENTS

INTRODUCTION   **5**

Student Safety, Academics, and Mental Health   8

How to Use This Book   11

How you will know the techniques are working:
What to expect in the classroom   13

**SECTION 1: BUILDING A SAFE ENVIRONMENT FOR
LEARNING AND SUPPORTING MENTAL HEALTH**   **19**

1. Greeting Students and Saying Goodbye   21

2. Introducing Myself   24

3. The Classroom Environment   26

4. Time for Questions   28

5. Saying Thank You   30

6. Participation   32

7. Language   37

8. Assignments and Curriculum   41

9. Mental-Health Check-In   45

Mental-Health Check List: Signs for Teachers to
Look for in the Classroom   49

Teacher Checklist   57

SECTION 2: MAINTAINING A SAFE ENVIRONMENT FOR LEARNING AND SUPPORTING MENTAL HEALTH   **59**

    1. Greeting Students and Saying Goodbye   61

    2. Classroom Environment   63

    3. Time for Questions   65

    4. Saying Thank You   67

    5. Participation   69

    6. Language   71

    7. Assignments and Curriculum   73

    8. Mental Health   75

    Teacher Checklist   79

SECTION 3: MOVING FORWARD FROM A SAFE ENVIRONMENT FOR LEARNING AND SUPPORTING MENTAL HEALTH BY TEACHING ASSERTIVENESS TECHNIQUES   **81**

    Lesson 1: Being Passive, Assertive, or Aggressive   83

    Lesson 2: Assertive Speaking   86

    Lesson 3: How to Say No   90

    Including Gardner's Multiple Intelligences in the Lessons   94

    Teacher Checklist   97

    Teacher Affirmations   99

Afterword   **101**

Endnotes   **103**

About the Author   **107**

INTRODUCTION

What everybody is looking to know is that when I walk into this space, when I speak to you, when I am present with you, that you see me, you hear me, and what I say matters. The truth is that every person you encounter is looking for that.

~ Oprah Winfrey

I've been a teacher for twenty-two years and when I first heard her say this, it resonated with me so much that I started to change the way I taught in my classroom. Oprah Winfrey's words apply universally and transcend gender, race, and class. Everyone, our students included, wants to feel this way, and I apply her advice to fit a classroom setting, to the way I teach my students, and to help explain the purpose behind the writing of this book. This is my version:

> *What every student wants to know is that when they walk into your classroom, when they speak to you, when they are present with you, that you see them, you hear them, and what they say matters to you. The truth is that every single student you encounter is looking for that, and your relationships with them improve exponentially when you get that that is what the students you teach are looking for.*

Over the years, as I've grown in multiple ways as a teacher, the overall goals in my classroom have changed. No longer do I feel that covering the curriculum is the main focus. I no longer go through the classroom "rules" at the start of the year. Instead, my main priority is to create a safe space for students to foster learning and confidence, and to support their overall mental health. At the beginning of the school year, I tell students that this is my main priority as their teacher and that together we will work towards our goal. I model how to act in the classroom, and students respond by mirroring my actions and behaviour. When the students leave my class at the end of the year and they tell me they felt safe and supported in class, I feel I have succeeded in a way that I don't feel when a student shares that they feel that they have mastered a curriculum concept. Not that student learning is not important to me, it definitely is, but I've learned that when I start from a place of creating a safe and supportive space in the classroom, a greater and deeper learning takes place for every student, and also for myself.

STUDENT SAFETY, ACADEMICS, AND MENTAL HEALTH

In my classroom I have noticed that when I can create a safe space where students feel they are seen and heard and that what they say matters, they improve academically. This doesn't mean that every student gets a certain mark or level; success is different for every student. What this does mean is that students show academic improvement. This can mean a higher mark, but it can also mean stronger literacy or numeracy skills or a personal feeling of having done well in the class. Having supports in place in a classroom regarding safety and mental health encourages students to take more risks, ask more questions, and share more ideas, and it increases their overall confidence and self-esteem, all of which results in more academic success. Sometimes colleagues would ask about a student they had taught in the past who was now in my class to see how they were doing.

Often my colleague was surprised when I shared how well the student was doing in my class. At first, I couldn't explain why, but after researching I found studies that show a link between feeling safe and supported in their classroom and academic success.

A 2016 study from Concordia University mirrors what I have found in my classroom. The study states that "good grades aren't just based on smarts—high marks also depend on a student's feeling of safety."[1] The opposite would also be true in that lower academic success by students is connected to a feeling of not being safe in a classroom environment. The same study goes on to state that "students who felt safer were more attentive and efficient in the classroom … and reported fewer symptoms of depression" and other mental health–related issues. Knowing this, teachers should aim to have their classrooms a safe space to support academic goals as well as positive mental health for all students at all levels and grades. In this way, the students will succeed in multiple ways in the classroom.

The CBC and the *Toronto Star* have reported that Black and Indigenous students have a higher suspension rate in the education system and face systemic racism that puts them at more of a disadvantage than other racial groups. These groups of students, along with other students of colour, LGBTQ+ students, students with special needs, and newcomers to Canada may not have felt seen or heard, or that what they say matters throughout their entire educational experience and deserve to have a teacher who can help them feel valued.

The COVID pandemic brought uncertainty and feelings of not being safe to both students and teachers. Disparities in education that existed before became more pronounced. It became harder to connect to students as we were forced to teach through a screen instead of in person. As teachers and students move into a post-pandemic learning environment, creating a safe space in the classroom where students feel seen and heard and that what they say matters is more important than ever to support both academic success and positive mental health.

HOW TO USE THIS BOOK

In the course of reading this book, you will learn how to show your students that you do see them, you do hear them, and that what they say matters to you. This can be done by following the techniques I've developed during my years of teaching and that I have found to work, so that by the end of the school year students are confident in their academic abilities, have more positive mental health, and are able to self-advocate throughout the rest of their educational journey.

Section 1, "Building a Safe Environment for Learning and Supporting Mental Health," covers the first part of the school year and introduces students to classroom routines that will create safety and a feeling of being seen and heard and that what they say matters. In this section I also include student voices by sharing what some of my own students have said about their experience in my classroom, having experienced the techniques outlined in the book.

Section 2, "Maintaining a Safe Environment for Learning and Supporting Mental Health," is done during the middle of the school year and maintains the classroom routines introduced in the Building Phase, ensuring that students continue to feel seen and heard and that what they say matters. This section also includes references to articles, studies, and research that supports the techniques I use in my classroom to show that there is evidence that the techniques work.

Section 3, "Teaching Assertiveness Techniques for Learning and Supporting Mental Health," is done in the last part of the school year, when students are taught valuable assertiveness and communication skills to self-advocate for their own sense of feeling seen and heard and that what they say matters once they leave your classroom. I also include mini-lessons that teachers can use to facilitate learning these skills, which can also be modified based on the individual teacher's grade and subject area.

I have used these techniques in my own classroom for years in many grades, levels, and subject areas with much success. My goal is that in sharing them, other teachers will also be able to make their classrooms safe spaces for students to succeed as well.

HOW YOU WILL KNOW
THE TECHNIQUES ARE WORKING:
WHAT TO EXPECT IN THE CLASSROOM

After reading this book you should feel prepared to implement the techniques in your own classroom, techniques that over the years I have found to be successful. Teachers may wonder how they will know that what they are doing is working. I will share what teachers can expect to happen in their classrooms based on my personal experiences with my students. Following are the results you can expect in your classroom when the techniques are working.

INCREASED PARTICIPATION

At the start of the year, I usually find student participation is fairly low. Yes, some students love to participate and do so right away, but many don't feel safe doing so yet at first, preferring not to participate in answering a question, reading aloud, or speaking during an online or in-person discussion.

Once you start to implement the techniques outlined in this book, one way you will know they are working is that you will see an increase in participation in the classroom. Students will be more willing to share their answers, read aloud, and speak during an online or in-person discussion. As students feel more seen and heard, and that what they say in the classroom matters, they will feel safer and want to participate in various ways. When you see this beginning to occur, you will know that what you are doing is working.

A STRONG SENSE OF COMMUNITY IN THE CLASSROOM

The start of the year is a "get to know you" phase for students and teachers. Community must be built, and sometimes it takes time for students and the teacher to feel comfortable with one another. Community is built on a foundation of students feeling that they are seen and heard, and that what they say matters.

Implementing the techniques in this book will expedite the building of a classroom community and do so in a stronger way because students will feel seen and heard and that what they say matters. A strong foundation is built in the classroom when students feel validated and safe. A strong classroom community may look as though students are engaging with each other in meaningful ways, supporting each other during class discussions online or in person, listening and responding to each other's ideas, and encouraging each other during presentations.

STUDENTS WILLING TO TAKE MORE RISKS ACADEMICALLY

When students don't feel that they are seen and heard, and that what they say matters in the classroom, I have found that they will want to protect themselves academically and personally. This results in their being quiet in the classroom, not asking many questions, and doing assignments in a way that shows that being "correct" is more important to them than taking a risk and possibly making a mistake and risking not learning something new.

By implementing the techniques in this book, a teacher can encourage more academic risk-taking. This will manifest as students asking more questions about a topic or assignment, going above and beyond in assignments, and/or asking for a more challenging topic.

I have also observed students asking me for help more often knowing that the help will be there for them if they decide to take on a new academic challenge. Making a "mistake" will be seen more as a learning experience than something to be ashamed of.

THE SHARING OF PERSONAL STORIES

Some students are naturally open and love to share information about themselves. However, not all students feel comfortable doing this. I have often had students who shared a lot of personal stories and information, whereas others shared nothing about themselves. When students feel seen and heard and that what they say matters, they are willing to share more about themselves in the classroom.

A teacher who uses the techniques outlined in this book will notice more students sharing personal stories and information about themselves with the teacher and their fellow students. This sharing adds valuable insight into class discussions and enables others to feel that they are not alone. When one student shares, others feel validated. Another thing teachers will notice is students supporting one another through verbal agreement or nodding in support when someone shares.

INCREASED STUDENT ACADEMIC ACHIEVEMENT

Even though I tell my students that marks are not of most importance, I find students often don't share my view. Learning takes a backseat to getting a "good" mark in the class. I find this outlook distances a student from the class because they are striving for only one outcome: a certain mark. Further, when a student doesn't feel safe and validated in the classroom, they will shut down. Shutting down doesn't result in academic success but, in fact, does the opposite. Shutting down can manifest as not completing assignments, not participating in class activities or discussions, and sometimes not attending class at all.

If a teacher implements the techniques in this book and creates a space where students feel seen and heard and that what they say matters, students will be more invested in the class and learning, which will result in academic success. Students will not shut down, but rather become more engaged with learning in the classroom, which will lead to more academic success. It is important to keep in mind that academic success will look different to each student and isn't linked to a certain grade. Since implementing these techniques in my classes, I noticed not only a rise in students' marks, but also that students viewed their marks in a more positive light, even if it wasn't the highest mark in the class.

BUILDING A SAFE ENVIRONMENT FOR LEARNING AND SUPPORTING MENTAL HEALTH

(First third of the school year)

I've always felt that, for teachers, the real "new year" is not in January but in September. The start of the school year is a hectic time in teaching and can bring up feelings of anxiety for students and teachers alike. Even after all my years in teaching, I still have anxiety dreams before I go back to school. For me, this is a good thing because it means I still have a lot invested in teaching—I care. If I didn't feel any nervous excitement at all, I'd worry.

The start of the school year brings unique challenges: meetings and reviewing the school's procedures, planning and prepping for classes, meeting new students, students meeting a new teacher, and everyone getting used to a new routine after being off for summer break. If teachers are also teaching online in some way, there are even more challenges to be tackled.

Yet, amid all these challenges, it is also the time of excitement and a time to begin to build a safe space in your classroom. This Building Phase starts for teachers on the days leading up to the first day of school, when teachers are preparing, and begins for students on the first day they attend school. The following will guide teachers on how to begin creating a safe space so that students feel seen and heard and that what they say matters.

1.
GREETING STUDENTS AND SAYING GOODBYE

Whether in person or online, greeting students is the first connection of the day that a teacher can make. Teachers shouldn't underestimate how much this means to students. A smile and hearing the teacher say hello to them using their name will enable students to feel seen in your classroom. Be sure to pronounce students' names as best you can on the first day of school so that they feel seen immediately. I have often reached out to other teachers to get the correct pronunciation of a name before school starts, and I write it down phonetically as a reference for myself on the first day of classes. I have also asked students privately to write their name phonetically for me or tell me how to pronounce it correctly before I take the attendance for the whole class. This way, I don't say a student's name incorrectly in front of the whole class.

When teaching in person, I'm always in my classroom before the students start to arrive. Will there be times when this is impossible? Yes. Having to prep something last minute happens to everyone, and you may not be in your classroom before students arrive every day, but overall, being in your classroom to greet students should be a priority. When teaching online, I made it a routine each day that each student say hello to me using their mic, or by typing their greeting in the chat area. I then acknowledged each of them by saying hello and saying their name.

If in-person, saying goodbye to students as they leave your classroom should also be a priority. Again, hearing the teacher say goodbye or have a good day using the students name is a way to make one last connection before they move to another class. I also left time at the end of our online sessions for students to say goodbye. I then said goodbye verbally to each student. The feedback I got from students was that this made them feel seen in a way that using an online attendance tracker couldn't.

Leaving time to greet students and say goodbye at the start and end of each class also allows space for students to approach you to ask a question, make a comment, or share something of interest. This may take time, but it is worth it because it creates a safer space in the classroom where students feel seen and heard and that what they say matters.

"It was fun to say hello and goodbye online!" LP

"I feel it's important to say hello and goodbye. It's nice to greet each other when we meet and leave." AM

2.
INTRODUCING MYSELF

On the first day of school when I introduce myself, I include my preferred pronouns. I do this to normalize the sharing of pronouns, and to let students know that our classroom is a safe space for them whatever their pronouns may be. Like many teachers, my go-to first day assignment is to have students write an introductory letter to me or complete a similar introductory activity. One of the things I ask students to include, if they feel comfortable, is their preferred pronouns. I've done this for years now, and have always received a positive response from students. Part of students' feeling seen and heard and that what they say matters in the classroom is giving them an opportunity to share their preferred pronouns and then respecting them throughout the year. Once you are aware of a student's preferred pronoun, it is also important to remember them as best you can. If you misgender a student, apologize and be mindful to remember next time. Recently, I started to refer to students primarily by their name or preferred name, and then use the more neutral pronoun of "they" in general.

"I am currently experimenting with pronouns at the moment, but for now she/her is totally fine." AQ

"I am fine with your referring to me by my name or cisgender pronouns, but honestly I'm fine with any pronouns also." CL

3.
THE CLASSROOM ENVIRONMENT

Just as a plant will flourish when given the right environment, so will students. Teachers should therefore think about what their classroom environment looks like. I realize much of the classroom environment may be out of a teacher's control, especially during COVID with distancing and other safety measures in place, but we can do what we can with what we have.

Posters on the wall should be inclusive, inspiring, and reflect the student population. In my classroom I have a Land Acknowledgement, a poster stating the classroom is a safe space for LGBTQ+ students and a Pride flag, along with some curriculum-specific posters. Student work should also be displayed to encourage the sharing of ideas and to show students that their work matters and is of value. Posters can be found in various places online, but I have found some great ones on Etsy; Amazon; and through the Scholastic website, as well as a site called Zazzle.

I also have a Bristol board with the title "Today I Am Grateful for ...," written on the top. Below the Bristol board I have sticky notes and a marker. Students are invited to write something on a sticky note and post it if they choose to do so. They don't have to include their name unless they feel comfortable to do so. To get things started, I always begin the Gratitude board post-it notes by writing that I am grateful for my classes that year. As the Bristol board fills up with gratitude during the school year, it adds to students' feeling seen and heard and that what they say matters. It also boosts the overall mood in the classroom to one of gratitude.

Finally, I have a desk in my classroom with supplies that I let students know they can use at any time. The supplies include hand sanitizer, Kleenex, a hole-punch, a stapler, and extra pens and pencils. Students don't have to ask to use these supplies; they are for them, and for our classroom community.

"The gratitude board made me happy to see it fill up during the year." CP

"I liked how I was able to display my very own mental health–week poster. ... It makes me feel proud our posters help some students identify what they were feeling." AF

4.

TIME FOR QUESTIONS

Having a routine in the way your class is set up brings a feeling of safety and predictability to students. Of course, every day in teaching is different and things may need to change at times, but having some set routines adds to the feeling of safety in the classroom and helps students feel seen and heard and that what they say matters.

One way I do this is to set aside time at the start, and the end, of class for any questions, concerns, worries, or comments. I usually leave ten minutes to do this. Students can ask about an assignment, things going on in our classroom, things going on in the school, or anything else on their minds. I find that having this space specifically for students to ask questions and for the teacher to answer them normalizes the asking of questions. Students can see that there is embedded time for them to voice their questions or comments, which emphasizes to them that their voices are a priority.

Of course, students can ask questions at any time during the class, and I normalize this by asking multiple times during a lesson if there are any questions. I also leave time after I answer for any other questions before I move on. Often students need a moment to think before they can articulate a question, and if the teacher doesn't wait and moves on too quickly, the student may decide not to ask at all instead of feeling as though they are interrupting the teacher who has moved on to the next topic. Besides asking for questions during the lesson, after the lesson is almost over, I walk around the classroom and ask each individual student if they have a question. Usually, students will ask more questions one-on-one than they would in a larger group setting. Both of these techniques make students feel seen and heard and that what they say matters.

"I don't have any questions today, Miss, but thank you for asking." HI

"I like knowing I can ask a question the next day during question time if I think of one during the night." VR

"I appreciate you answering my questions even though I ask too many, hahaha." DM

5.
SAYING THANK YOU

I've been told by students that I'm a very polite teacher. To me, this is the greatest compliment. I make sure to thank students all the time—for participating in class, for reading aloud, for pointing out when I've made a mistake, for doing their homework, for completing assignments on time, and for a myriad of other things that students do in a classroom.

When I shared this with colleagues, I sometimes got a confused reaction. They ask why I would thank students for doing what they are, in fact, expected to do. I agree that many of the things I thank students for are part of being a successful student, but I thank them because I'm honestly grateful that they are doing what they are expected to do. It makes my life easier as a teacher, and adds to the overall community feeling in the classroom as we all work towards the same end goal of the various definitions of student success.

Let's take the example of completing a homework assignment. When I check homework, I thank each student who has completed it as I go around the room to check. I'm grateful because this saves my having to follow up, to perhaps make contact with an adult at home, and because often the lesson that day is better when students have completed the homework assigned. I also thank students to validate them, to show them that I see that they did their homework and appreciate it, and that what they do matters to me. I find that when I do this in the classroom, the number of students who complete their homework increases in the first part of the year and then remains steady for the rest of the year. The consistent positive feedback students receive when they complete assigned tasks shows them they are seen and heard and that what they say matters through the work that they complete.

"I feel happy and confident in class!" OK

"Thank YOU, Ms. Alexander!" AM

6.

PARTICIPATION

I think teachers would agree that class participation is key to a successful classroom environment. We've all had years when we have a quieter class in relation to participation, and it can make teaching much more challenging. I have learned to encourage participation in my classroom in a way that ensures students feel safe to participate and builds student confidence at the same time. I find using the following technique ensures that participation increases steadily throughout the year and helps to create community in the classroom.

I let students know on the first day of class that I will never do the following: I will never call on a student to read aloud if they don't have their hand up to do so; I tell them that if they do offer to read, they can read as much as they want and then stop; and I tell them that

I will never make a student share an answer verbally or by writing it on the board without being given the opportunity to first check with me that their answer is correct. This immediately puts the whole class at ease. I know there are some teachers who feel that calling on students to answer a question or read aloud who don't want to is a good thing and that if a student is "caught" unprepared, then in future they will make sure they are prepared for class. I strongly disagree. When students are put on the spot, unprepared to read or answer aloud, or give an incorrect answer, their confidence and self-esteem suffer. Shaming and embarrassing a student does not make a student feel safe in the classroom and does not make them feel seen and heard and that what they say matters. Instead, students will shut down and not be encouraged or motivated to be prepared next time. I believe a classroom should be a place of building confidence and self-esteem in students and my initial announcement to my classes on participation does just that.

I further make participation safe by giving positive feedback when students do participate and thank them for doing so. When I check homework, I will point out an answer that is correct and ask that student if they would mind sharing it when we discuss the answers that day. If the student says no, I respect that, but they usually are more willing to share because they have been told their answer is of value and correct. They feel seen and heard and know that what they say matters. When I can point out an answer that is correct day after day, students' confidence in their work increases and soon they are more willing to participate without my having to tell them their work is correct. Students begin to see their own value instead of looking to the teacher to validate them.

Similarly, when I ask if anyone would like to write an answer or idea on the board, I tell them they can check their answer with me first if they wish. I always give positive feedback, and if their answer is incorrect, I ask them to modify it before they put it on the board. Alternatively, I privately tell the student why their answer is incorrect and have a brief discussion about what the correct answer is, and then they can write that answer on the board. Pointing out that there is more than one "correct" answer is also key to building a safe classroom environment. More students will share when they know there is more than one option for an answer or idea. They can still be "correct" even if their answer is different from that of another student. Students feel safe to share an answer on the board because they know it is correct, and this way, in the end the board is filled with correct answers, which makes the activity easier to take up and discuss as a class.

At the start of the year—the Building Phase, almost every student asks me to check their work before they share or write something on the board. But soon this changes. As students realize that they are for the most part always correct, their confidence builds. As time goes by, fewer and fewer students feel they need me to check their answers as they are confident that they are correct. More students offer to read aloud or verbally share an answer because they know that it is their choice and they can read as much as they want and stop when they want. Students are empowered and feel seen and heard and that what they say matters because they can see that it actually does through the daily measures taken by the teacher in the classroom.

Finally, I tell students that participation can also be something as simple as raising their hand. This allows them to feel seen and heard and that what they say matters, even if they are quieter than other students. When one student answers out loud, I give positive feedback and then I ask the rest of the class to raise their hands if they had the same, or a similar answer. All students are given the opportunity to participate in this way, further building confidence. This also gives me an idea as a teacher if the class as a whole understands the concept or idea being taught. There have been times when very few students have the same or similar answer, and then I have the opportunity as a teacher to go through the concept again to ensure understanding and future student success.

"Thank you for creating a safe space for us in class where we feel comfortable to open up." JS

"With the help of my teacher, Ms. Alexander, in looking over my work and providing reliable feedback and information it got me to build the momentum to try my best and overcome my difficulties." BC

"I appreciate you for understanding that some people are not as outgoing as others and do not always want to share their ideas." AG

7.
LANGUAGE

What a teacher says matters more than many of us realize. When I've asked students to recall a negative comment a teacher made to them, they all have many to share, some remembering a comment a teacher made years ago. These comments, many made offhandedly by a teacher, become mistaken beliefs in students. A mistaken belief is something that someone believes about themselves, not because it is true, but because someone once made a negative comment to them that was taken as truth. For example: I have students who believe they are "not good at English," not because that is the truth but because a past teacher told them they weren't. This mistaken belief stays with the student and becomes a negative self-fulfilling prophecy. First, a teacher makes a negative comment to a student. The student then believes the comment because it is being made by someone who is an authority figure in their eyes. Then the student isn't successful in the class because they don't believe they can be. Students' self-esteem suffers from negative comments made in the classroom and this harms them in many ways and for years to come.

Also, using negative comments towards an individual student, or the class as a whole, is not a classroom-management technique. Students do not respond to being told they are "stupid," "at the wrong level," or the like. Instead, they shut down because they don't feel seen and heard or that what they say matters. Using supportive, nonviolent communication in the classroom is key in creating a safe space where students feel valued. Tone of voice is also something to be mindful of since students pick up on whether a teacher's tone of voice matches their words.

In my classroom I constantly tell my students they are smart, that their assignments are great, that they can master a challenging concept, and that they can succeed. What I've discovered is that when positive and supportive language is used in the classroom, students feel more positive and supported and succeed more both socially and academically in class.

Some of the nonviolent communicative phrases I use verbally or written on assignments as feedback include:

"This looks great! I just have a few suggestions …"

"Thank you for handing in your work. What do you think about making a few changes that I can suggest?"

"I loved your ideas! Could we work together to make them clearer?"

"This is so creative, I'm impressed! Your format could improve a bit, can I help you with that?"

"Great work! I think you might not have completely understood my instructions, though. Will you let me clarify them with you so you can make some changes before I evaluate this?"

From the few examples above, you can see I always start with a positive, and very gently invite the student to make the needed changes to their work. I find students are more willing to make changes and listen to clarification or further instructions when they don't feel that they are being told they did something wrong. I also try to ask for permission to help the student and make suggestions on how to improve to make sure the student feels empowered and as though they are being seen and heard and that what they say matters, even when I am correcting or editing their work. If a student says they don't want to make changes or accept help, then the teacher needs to honour that and perhaps later remind the student that help was offered but refused. Even though I am correcting errors, I make sure my overall tone in feedback is positive. There is always something good to say, a skill that the student has mastered, that they handed in the work on time, tried their best, or something else that garners praise. Focusing on the positive before making a correction also makes students more open to suggestions on how to improve on their work.

> *"You showed our class so much kindness and never wanted to make any student feel upset or uncomfortable." AG*

> *"Thank you for putting your students as your main priority and concern." MF*

8.
ASSIGNMENTS AND CURRICULUM

The curriculum in a course is mandated by the government and often outside of a teacher's control. However, as long as teachers are covering the curriculum, the assignments we do and the resources we use can be more individualized. Through assignments and resources, teachers can create a classroom where students feel seen and heard and that what they say matters.

Teachers are all familiar with Howard Gardner's Multiple Intelligences theory as it is taught in all teacher-training programs in Canada. Keeping Garner's eight intelligences in mind—Linguistic, Logical/Mathematical, Spatial, Bodily/Kinesthetic, Musical, Interpersonal, Intrapersonal, and Naturalistic—is important when creating lessons and assignments to be evaluated. If, over the course of the school year, teachers allow students to explore their intelligence strengths they will not only succeed academically but also feel more seen and heard and that what they say matters because they can express themselves in ways that are natural to them as an individual student.

Besides the eight intelligences, the students' voices should be at the core of every lesson and assignment. Giving options is something I do in my classroom as often as I can. If I do a lesson I will include a written note, a YouTube video, an activity where students can get up and move around, a way for students to self-reflect, and a way for them to talk to others and share ideas. If I do an assignment, I try to give multiple ways to complete the assignment, to allow students to choose the character or book to focus on, to include a creative component to their work, to record or film their assignment, and I will even provide the class with multiple due dates, and we discuss as a class when the assignment should be due. Choice, even a small one, allows a more personal connection to be made between student and subject.

The types of resources used in the classroom also play a critical role in students feeling seen and heard and that what they say matters. Representation is key to student success, and so having a diverse curriculum of poems, stories, books, films, articles, and podcasts from a variety of authors of diverse backgrounds is necessary.

Further, to empower students and make them feel safer in the classroom as often as I can, as a class we will come up with a due date for assignments. Of course, this doesn't always happen as sometimes teachers will have set deadlines that need to be met, but most of the time due dates can be decided on as a class. I find that when I do this, students hand in their work on time more often, fewer students ask for more time to complete their work, and they feel seen and heard and that what they say matters. For example, I once had an English class where many of the students were also in the same Science class. When I had a due-date discussion with my class for our writing assignment, I learned that half of my class had a Science test the next week. Together, we were able to discuss and come up with a due date for our assignment that worked for most students. Students were able to manage the workload, I got all the assignments in on time, and everyone felt good about the situation.

When students feel they have choice and some control in the assignments and due dates, and see themselves and their stories represented in the curriculum, they will feel more seen and heard and that what they say matters.

"I've really enjoyed exploring new stories through different mediums, like the Finding Cleo podcast." IB

"I liked how 'The Hate U Give' was a blend of curriculum and social justice issues ... it was more applicable to real life." MF

"I appreciated how what we learned [The Hate U Give] could be connected to our present-day society." MS

"I mean that for most teenagers and people books aren't the primary source of entertainment, but I do think that when teachers pick books like The Hate U Give to read in class it makes a huge difference because these kids want to read the book." NL

9.
MENTAL-HEALTH CHECK-IN

Mental health has become a word heard quite a lot during the COVID pandemic, especially its importance in the classroom. Yet I find concrete ways to support students' mental health in the classroom are few and far between. I've been doing a mental-health check-in at the start of my classes for years. It became more invaluable teaching during the pandemic and contributed to a safe classroom environment where students feel seen and heard and that what they say matters.

I post pieces of chart paper with positive-feeling words, neutral-feeling words, and one with negative-feeling words in my classroom. From the first day of class I invite students to think about how they are feeling that day and select one or two words to share. They can also think of their own word that may not be on the chart, and then I add that word for future use. Alternatively, students can share a number from one to ten on their overall mood. Students are told they don't have to explain why they chose the word or number, but they can if they wish to. I always start and participate in the sharing of my words.

Examples of Positive-Feeling Words to Post and Share

Worthy	Energetic	Excited	Fulfilled
Alert	Eager	Grateful	Optimistic
Peaceful	Happy	Encouraged	Relieved
Proud	Inspired	Hopeful	Relaxed
Incredible	Confident	Safe	Joyous

Examples of Neutral-Feeling Words to Post and Share

Mellow	Neutral	Just OK	Quiet
Preoccupied	Calm	Relaxed	Uninterested
Blah	Complacent	Apathetic	Distracted
Satisfied	Indifferent	Hesitant	Bored
Lazy	Tired	Reserved	Nonchalant

Examples of Negative-Feeling Words to Post and Share

Scared	Pessimistic	Overwhelmed	Frustrated
Angry	Anxious	Annoyed	Worried
Confused	Disappointed	Stressed	Helpless
Lonely	Nervous	Hurt	Panicked
Sad	Restless	Impatient	Exasperated

This check-in allows me to do two things. First, it allows me to see the general mood of the class. If the general mood is leaning towards the negative, for example the stress of exams, I can follow up and we can have a class discussion on how to manage the stress. If the words are mostly positive, then we can celebrate as a class the joy that we're feeling. Next, this check-in allows me to see how individual students are feeling. If I notice a student sharing a negative word who usually doesn't, I can follow up with them privately, asking if they would like to share more and how I can help. If I notice a student regularly sharing more negative words, I can also follow up with them privately and perhaps refer them to a school support to help. Also, I can follow up with students who share positive words and ask them what is making them feel joy in their lives at that moment, and we can celebrate that together.

This quick way to start the class provides a lot of information to a teacher, allows students to see that others feel the same way they do, and supports the goal of students being seen and heard and feeling that what they say matters. In the transitioning between in-person and online learning during COVID, the check-in and sharing of words was also a much-needed way to express the frustration and disappointment we were all feeling, and to feel supported by others. How much did students depend on this daily sharing of words? In one instance in the chaos of transitioning back and forth so many times between online and in-person learning, I forgot to ask a class to share their words. To my delight, after class I received many emails from students letting me know that I had forgotten, and they shared their word for that day. I replied, with a smile on my face, to each student, thanking them for sharing, sharing my own word with them, and promising not to forget that part of our day again.

> *"It always helps to know that there is someone who checks in on you and offers clarity during the most uncertain of times. ... Thank you for helping me realize the importance of mental health and taking time for yourself." NS*

> *"The mental-health check-ins were genius." MB*

MENTAL-HEALTH CHECK LIST: SIGNS FOR TEACHERS TO LOOK FOR IN THE CLASSROOM

Teachers are not doctors, nor are they trained to recognize mental-health issues in our students. However, as a classroom teacher we are often the first person who might recognize such an issue in a student and be the first contact of help and referral to a school support worker. According to a study done by Sick Kids Hospital in Toronto,[2] during the COVID pandemic the number of students who are struggling with issues such as Anxiety Disorder, Depression, Obsessive Compulsive Disorder, Self-Harm, and eating disorders "heightened and will have serious, sustained negative impact" on students. Black students, Indigenous students, newcomers to Canada, students with special needs, LGBTQ+ students, and students of colour are even more at risk in the classroom regarding mental health. Below I list some of the most common mental-health disorders and some signs teachers can look for in their classrooms so they can refer the student to a school support, such as a guidance counsellor, an administrator, the school social worker, the school psychologist, or the child-and-youth worker. All information, and more, can be found on the website of the Centre for Addiction and Mental Health (CAMH). After the common signs to look for, I list some conditions to look for that have appeared in my classroom that could be indicators of a mental-health issue.

ANXIETY DISORDER

- Irrational fears not appropriate for the situation at hand
- Decline in memory
- Inability to be flexible and resistant to changes in the classroom routine
- Avoidance of situations or doing school work
- Anxiety or Panic Attacks consisting of a racing heart, upset stomach, headaches, and difficulty breathing

Possible Examples of Anxiety in the Classroom

- Irrational fears over a test, assignment, or activity

- A student not remembering information even though you are sure a student knows the information, or forgetting a classroom routine

- An inappropriate reaction to a change in the daily routine or environment

- Not completing assignments or tasks for no apparent reason

- Student expressing physical symptoms when they are not physically ill

DEPRESSION

- Student becomes withdrawn

- Fatigue

- Difficulty making decisions

- Decline in memory

- Loss of interest in activities

Possible Examples of Depression in the Classroom

- A student becoming more withdrawn than usual for an extended period of time
- A student falling asleep in class or expressing fatigue for an extended period of time
- Struggling to make a decision that would not usually take long to make
- Struggling to remember academic or classroom routines when the student didn't have trouble before
- A change in interest in activities the student was formerly interested in and excited about

OBSESSIVE COMPULSIVE DISORDER

- Performing repetitive compulsive behaviours
- Obsession on a certain topic
- Inability to be flexible or accept change
- Anxiety when compulsive behaviours cannot be performed
- Anxiety or panic attacks

Possible Examples of Obsessive-Compulsive Disorder in the Classroom

- Seeing the student perform repetitive actions in the classroom, at lunch, at recess, or the student asking to leave the classroom often to be able to perform the compulsion

- A student's obsession with a certain topic where they will ask excessive questions about it or not be able to think about another topic even to do an assignment or activity

- An overreaction to any change in the daily classroom routine

- An overreaction when a student is asked not to perform their compulsion or are not given permission to leave the classroom to do so

- Frequent anxiety or panic attacks

EATING DISORDERS

- Preoccupation with food
- Preoccupation with body size and weight
- Routines and rituals around food and eating
- Obsessive activity
- Anxiety when food routines and activity cannot be performed

Examples of Eating Disorders in the Classroom

- Student talking about food often or a preoccupation with food
- Student talking about body image often or a preoccupation with body image by comparing themselves to others
- When a student eats, they have various rules or rituals around food, such as eating only at a certain time, eating only certain foods, or eating foods in a certain order
- Having some of the signs of obsessive-compulsive disorder that involve food, eating, and body image
- Having anxiety arise when one of the food rituals can't be performed, or a fear of eating certain foods

SELF-HARMING

- Visible self-harming such as cuts or scratches on the body
- Not being able to explain any visible self-harming seen on the body
- Wearing clothing to cover any self-harm even when inappropriate for the weather
- Depression or anxiety
- Scars from previous self-harming

Examples of Self Harm in the Classroom

- Seeing cuts or scratches on a student's body
- When asked, a student cannot explain how they hurt themselves, or their explanation doesn't make sense
- A student wearing long sleeves and long pants in the classroom even when not appropriate for the weather and not being willing to change into more appropriate clothing
- The signs of Depression and Anxiety that can lead to self-harm
- Seeing scars on the student's body that appear excessive

Overall, a teacher should be mindful of any changes in a student's behaviours throughout the school year. Physical, mental, emotional, or academic changes that seem more than just the usual changes a student might experience are things to look for. A teacher should then refer the student to a school support in order to help the student and receive more direction on what to do in the classroom. A large part of students' feeling seen and heard and that what they say matters includes acknowledging and validating students' mental health along with providing the appropriate referral and supports needed for the student to feel safe and continue to be successful in the classroom.

The Building Phase can be difficult for both teacher and student to get used to, especially if this is the first time implementing these techniques into the classroom. Even if you feel it isn't working, I encourage teachers to stick with it; it will work in time. Trust the process of building a safe classroom where students feel seen and heard and that what they say matters.

Moving forward you will maintain what you have built in the second part of the school year and prepare students to leave your class with more confidence than when they arrived, knowing that they are of value.

TEACHER CHECKLIST

☐ Are you prepared to say hello and goodbye to your students each day?

☐ Have you prepared your first day's introduction, including sharing your pronouns?

☐ Does the classroom have diverse posters on display?

☐ Does the classroom have a Land Acknowledgement and a LGBTQ+ poster on display?

☐ Is there a space ready to display student work in the classroom?

☐ Is the Gratitude Board set up in the class and ready for use?

☐ Are there supplies such as Kleenex, hand sanitizer, a stapler, and hole-punch available for students to use?

☐ Is there time for questions embedded in lesson plans?

☐ Are diverse resources prepared and ready to use in daily lessons?

☐ Are the mental-health words posted where students can see them to use each day?

MAINTAINING A SAFE ENVIRONMENT FOR LEARNING AND SUPPORTING MENTAL HEALTH

(Middle of the school year)

Moving into the second part, the Maintenance Phase, of the school year, routines have been established and teachers and students know each other better. The Building Phase has been a success, and as a teacher you will see more confidence in your students and a strong community being created in the classroom. Students will feel safe and know that they are seen and heard and that what they say matters.

Maintaining all the hard work both teacher and student have done since the school year began is important. A consistency in teaching style also adds to students feeling safe in the classroom environment.

1.
GREETING STUDENTS AND SAYING GOODBYE

Even though the school year gets busier at the mid-way point, it's important to continue to greet students before class and say goodbye to them at the end of class. Students will continue to feel seen because they are acknowledged by name when they enter the classroom and again at the end of class when they leave. Students will also feel heard because a simple greeting or goodbye leaves space for a student to connect with the teacher to make a comment, share a story, or just to share a smile. Finally, students will feel that what they say matters because there is time embedded in the class for hellos and goodbyes.

The article "Brené Brown on How Gratitude Begets Joy"[3] supports the importance of greeting and saying goodbye to students and outlines that doing this daily communicates to students that they matter and are welcome, that you as a teacher are here and are not going anywhere, that the interaction of saying hello and goodbye matters, that the teacher cares about community, and that the teacher is accessible.

Further to being accessible as a teacher, in the Building Phase I include introducing myself. Of course, a teacher needs to introduce themselves to the class only once as by the midpoint of the year, hopefully teachers know all their students' names, how to say them correctly, and each student's preferred pronoun. In the Maintenance Phase it is also important for teachers to be open to any changes a student might make in the pronoun they prefer you use. The start and the end of class, when you greet and say goodbye to your students may be the time when a student may share their new pronoun with you, so again they feel seen and heard and that what they say matters.

2.
CLASSROOM ENVIRONMENT

Making sure the supplies such as a hole-puncher, stapler, Kleenex, and now hand sanitizer, are always available and replenished when in a physical classroom; this should be done so students can count on having them available when needed. Also, displaying student work in the physical or online classroom can, and should, be done throughout the year. The posters in the room can reflect a certain unit or theme and make the space more interesting and representative of the students themselves.

An article entitled "Responsive Classroom: Displaying Student Work"[4] supports the idea of displaying motivational posters and student work by saying that doing so sends a message to students that their work and learning is important. This, of course, adds to students feeling seen and heard and that what they say matters.

The Gratitude Board in my classroom always really starts to fill up by the midpoint of the year. I make sure to keep markers and sticky notes available for students to post what they are grateful for. In the Maintenance Phase I will make reference to the board, pointing out how full it's getting, what people have posted about, or if something happens in the classroom that we're all grateful for, and I ask if anyone wants to post on the board. This is actively practising gratitude.

The author and speaker Brené Brown stated in an interview that not just being grateful but participating in the practice of gratitude brings joy, and what teacher wouldn't want more joy in their classroom every day?[3] The Gratitude Board is an easy way to achieve this in the classroom and will work for every grade, level, and subject area.

3.
TIME FOR QUESTIONS

In the Building Phase, I made time available at the start and end of each class for questions, comments, concerns, or worries. Pre-COVID, there were times of the year when students had a lot to say—and times when they did not. During COVID, however, every single day I was met with many questions, comments, concerns, and worries. If I couldn't answer a question at that moment, I would get the answer and let the student or the class know as soon as I could. I was also honest about questions that I didn't know the answer to. Sitting in the uncertainty of COVID with the students allowed us to have the connection of being vulnerable. As a teacher, I could then discuss ways to handle this uncertainty with the students, which helped to support positive mental health.

Students knew this time for questions was going to be available every day. Setting this time aside should be maintained as the school year goes on and gets busier. It shows students that any questions, comments, worries, or concerns they have are important and valid. When a student expresses something during this time, I always make sure to comment that the question was a great one, that their comment makes a good point, or that their worry or concern is one that others probably have too. Sometimes I will ask others to raise their hands if they also had the same point, worry, or concern, further validating the student who first spoke and creating an even stronger classroom community. Having this time embedded into the class allows students to feel seen and heard and that what they say matters.

This is supported by an article titled "Encouraging Students to Ask Questions," where the author states the importance of creating a safe space for students to ask questions.[5] The author also states that praising students' questions will encourage and normalize the asking of questions. Removing the stigma around the asking of questions benefits the class as a whole because, I believe, the more questions that are asked the more opportunities there are to learn.

4.
SAYING THANK YOU

Continuing to thank students, even for doing the every-day things that all successful students do, is something a teacher should continue to do in the second phase of the school year. As the year goes on and gets busier, I find myself more grateful that students are completing work, handing in assignments on time, participating in class, correcting me when I make a mistake, and other things that add to the overall positive classroom environment. So of course, I continue to thank students whenever I can.

This modelling of thanking students is also returned as many students also begin to thank me more often. This reciprocal gratitude supports a safe classroom and makes students feel seen and heard and that what they say matters, which is the overall goal for the year.

An article titled "Why 'Thank You' is More Than Just Good Manners," the author states that "being grateful can improve well-being, physical health, can strengthen social relationships, produce positive emotional states and help us cope with stressful times in our lives."[6] Thanking students consistently in the classroom can produce all of these effects and create a safe classroom environment in the process.

Further, the author says that saying thank you is also important "because we want the other person to know we value what they've done for us and, maybe, encourage them to help us again in the future."[6] In the context of a classroom, an example of this could be the completing of homework or other assignments. Thanking students for completing a homework assignment shows them that the teacher values what they have done, thus encouraging them to continue to complete their homework or other assignments in the future.

5.
PARTICIPATION

As explained in the Building Phase of the school year, I always tell my students that I will never do the following: I will never call on a student to read aloud if they don't have their hand up to do so; I will never call on a student to answer a question if they don't have their hand up; I will never make a student read aloud if they don't want to, and if they do read they can read as much as they want and stop when they want; and I will never make a student share an answer verbally or by writing it on the board without first giving them the opportunity to check with me first to see that their answer correct. By the end of the Building Phase students feel safe to participate in various ways on their own, knowing that it is their choice to do so. As the year moves to the Maintenance Phase, it is important for the teacher to keep up this practice so students continue to feel safe to participate in ways that are comfortable for them.

And further related to thanking students, I continue to thank those who do participate and continue with the technique of raising a hand or liking someone's comment in an online chat. Student confidence will continue to be built in the Maintenance Phase, making them feel seen and heard and that what they say matters.

In an article titled "Encouraging Class Participation," the author calls class participation "an important aspect of student learning" and goes further to say that when students participate, they "learn to express their ideas in a way that others can understand. ... [T]hey learn how to obtain information to enhance their own learning of a topic."[7] For students to achieve this important aspect of learning they must first feel safe to participate in the first place. If students don't feel that they will be seen and heard and that what they say matters when they participate, they won't do it. The practice of not forcing students to participate brings a level of safety to participation that students will respond to positively.

6.
LANGUAGE

In the Building Phase, a teacher should be using positive, nonviolent, and supportive language when speaking to the class. This will build student confidence, support the creation of a space for everyone in the classroom, and begin to aid students in dismantling any mistaken beliefs they have due to past negative comments made to them by teachers. Again, putting students down is not a classroom-management technique, and students will shut down if spoken to in a demeaning way or if they feel shamed or embarrassed. This is the opposite of what a safe classroom where students feel seen and heard and that what they say matters looks like.

As concepts in the curriculum become more challenging as the school year goes on, it is important to be consistent in telling students that they are smart, that they can succeed, that their answers are insightful, and that their assignments are well done and insightful. Positive verbal interactions between teacher and student every day is important in helping the students feel that they are seen and heard and that what they say matters. Gentle corrections when errors occur, with a focus on what was done correctly, further fosters a student's self-esteem and creates a safe classroom environment. The Responsive Classroom website posted an article entitled, "Want Positive Behavior? Use Positive Language," which supports this point. The article says that when a teacher uses positive language in the classroom it can show "your belief in children's abilities and intentions [and] help them internalize a positive identity."[8] The article also supports what I do in the classroom regarding the benefits of finding positives that can be named in all students. Even students who are struggling with curriculum or social skills in the classroom have something positive about them that a teacher can notice and mention. Students who struggle in either of these ways need to feel seen and heard and that what they say matters even more.

7.

ASSIGNMENTS AND CURRICULUM

When students see themselves reflected in the curriculum they are learning, they are more engaged. Students will feel seen and heard and that what they say matters when what they are reading, viewing, hearing, and learning relates to them personally.

Even if the curriculum itself is outside a teacher's control because it is mandated, how a teacher teaches that curriculum can be diverse and focus on students' voices and experiences. Giving students choices in assignments, due dates, and resources to be used creates a sense of validation, ownership of learning, and student engagement. An engaged student will be more successful in the classroom.

A Government of Ontario document entitled "Human Rights, Equity, and Inclusive Education" outlines the importance of diversity in the classroom and even links its importance to Human Rights. The document states that the education system "must respect diversity, promote inclusive education, and work towards identifying and eliminating barriers to equal treatment in education that limit the ability of students to learn, grow, and contribute to society." Assignments and resources a teacher use should do the same. The document goes on to state that teachers should "give students a variety of opportunities to learn about diversity and diverse perspectives ... and by creating opportunities for their experiences to be affirmed and valued ... [to] see themselves reflected in the curriculum. It is essential that learning activities and materials used to support the curriculum reflect the diversity of Ontario society."[9]

In other words, a classroom where students feel seen and heard and that what they say matters is a human right that teachers should be providing. Sadly, I know there are still many course syllabi where the focus is still based on the white colonial voice. This needs to change and the individual classroom teacher can take concrete steps to do this.

8.
MENTAL HEALTH

Continuing to do the daily mental-health check-in during the Maintenance Phase with the class will provide valuable information for teacher and student alike. As the year goes on and things get busy, I can see, as the teacher, what the overall mood of the class is and address any concerns. Further, the students can see that they are not alone in any anxiety that arises throughout the year, which creates a safe space in the classroom. This short daily activity enables students to feel seen and heard and that what they say matters in terms of their mental health. It also allows a teacher to continue to refer students to school support workers if the need arises. Again, a change in student behaviour could be something to look for regarding a mental-health issue that might arise, as well as the signs and symptoms to look for in the classroom as outlined in the Building Phase of this book.

Having the words posted allows students to learn how to express how they are feeling, and not having to provide an explanation in front of the rest of the class, unless they want to, creates a safe space to share. There have been times when I've noticed the level of anxiety in the class rise, so I then plan for a "Mental Health Day" for the class and myself. This is a day when I don't plan a lesson but instead allow students to catch up on our class work; catch up on other work; or even draw, read, or take a nap. Colleagues I have shared this with have often commented that students must take advantage of these mental-health days as an excuse to not do course work. This is a negative and stereotypical view of students. In fact, I've found just the opposite, and see students use this day to do things that they feel will best support their mental health. Sometimes it is to catch up on work for our class or another class, read a book, connect with others, speak to a school support worker, or a combination of these. It is important that when students say they are struggling mentally, that teachers listen so the students see that they are seen and heard and that what they say matters.

The School Mental Health Ontario (SMHO) explains that educators "have a significant influence on students' lives. The relationships you develop with students aren't just about academics. [Teachers are] a trusted and caring adult, and an ideal person to help them learn about and care for their mental health."[10]

I have personally seen that students who feel safe in a classroom and that they are seen and heard and that what they say matters will excel more than when they do not feel this way. The SMHO site supports this and expands by saying, "positive mental health is foundational to academic achievement, life skills, and overall wellbeing. The efforts [teachers] make to support your student's mental health will have an impact now and, in the future," which is exactly what teachers should strive to achieve.

The daily check in activity also breaks down the stigma surrounding mental health, normalizing talking about mental health. It also expands students' vocabulary regarding feelings, and encourages students to reach out if they need to. All of these are referenced by the SMHO site as how educators can support student mental health.[10]

As the end of the school year gets closer, the Maintenance Phase nears its end. Students will feel seen and heard and that what they say matters due to the work the teacher—and the students—have done in the first two phases. Moving forward to the last part of the year, students will be prepared to leave class with more confidence than when they arrived, knowing that they are of value, which they learned throughout the school year. In the final phase of the year students will learn concrete skills for being assertive so that when they leave class, they can self-advocate and continue to feel seen and heard and that what they say matters in other classes.

TEACHER CHECKLIST

☐ Have you continued to make time to say hello and goodbye to students each day?

☐ Are there still diverse posters on display in the classroom?

☐ Are the Land Acknowledgement and LGBTQ+ posters still on display?

☐ Is the Gratitude Board available and being used by teacher and students?

☐ Are the supplies that students may need refreshed and available for use?

☐ Is time for questions still embedded into the daily lesson plan?

☐ Are diverse resources being used in the daily lesson plans?

☐ Are the mental-health check-in words still posted and students asked daily to share a word?

MOVING FORWARD FROM A SAFE ENVIRONMENT FOR LEARNING AND SUPPORTING MENTAL HEALTH BY TEACHING ASSERTIVENESS TECHNIQUES

(Last third of the school year)

Even though the end of the school year is very busy, my years of teaching have also shown me that there are days that can be used to prepare students to move on to the next learning environment. In the last phase, the Assertive Phase, of creating a classroom where students feel seen and heard and that what they say matters, I prepare students to be assertive and self-advocate, and to use the skills I have been using in the classroom for themselves. This will further empower students and they can then take with them the feelings of safety and confidence that they felt in my classroom to a new classroom or environment.

Below I outline the main skills I teach near the end of my class and provide a mini-lesson to teach many ways to be assertive. When I teach these lessons in my classroom, they are much more detailed and are tailored to my individual class. The mini-lessons are more general, and teachers can adapt them based on their grade level and unique classroom needs, but this gives teachers a place to start.

LESSON 1:
BEING PASSIVE, ASSERTIVE,
OR AGGRESSIVE

Rationale: Students may not know these words but they would have acted in each of these ways at some point in their lives. One component to students' feeling seen and heard and that what they say matters is the ability to know the differences between being passive, assertive, and aggressive. Also, to be aware of which way they tend to express themselves in their lives and how to move towards a more assertive communication skill set.

LEARNING OUTCOMES:

After this lesson students will be able to do the following:

- Define the words passive, assertive, and aggressive formally and in their own words
- Reflect and share their own experiences of being passive, assertive, or aggressive
- Recognize the pros and cons of acting in a passive, assertive, and/or aggressive manner

MINI LESSON STEPS:

- The teacher should lead a brainstorm activity of the words "Passive," "Assertive," and "Aggressive" with the class.
- The teacher can facilitate a class discussion on the formal definitions of each word appropriate to the grade and level of the students.
- Next, the teacher can ask students to think of a time when they had been passive, assertive, or aggressive in their own lives. Students can share their experiences in a way the teacher feels fits the specific class and students, such as: self-reflection, journal response, a think-pair-share activity, a full class discussion, or an online post or discussion.

- Finally, the teacher can lead a class discussion on the pros and cons of being passive, assertive, and aggressive with the class. Again, students can share their ideas in any way the teacher feels is appropriate to the class, such as: self-reflection, journal response, a think-pair-share activity, a full class discussion, an online post or discussion, or creating a class chart on the board or screen.

LESSON 2:
ASSERTIVE SPEAKING

Rationale: Students may not know how to speak assertively and will learn how to do so in this lesson. Another component to students feeling seen and heard and that what they say matters is to know how to speak assertively in their own lives to self-advocate for their needs. Assertiveness speaking fosters confidence in students and they will be able to express themselves in a non-violent way to get their needs fulfilled.

LEARNING OUTCOMES:

After this lesson, students will be able to do the following:

- Use the assertive-speaking template to come up with an assertive-speaking statement based on age- and grade-specific scenarios.

- Reflect on a time in their lives when they wished they had been more assertive but weren't able to be, and create a personal assertive-speaking statement they could have used.

- Think of a current situation where they feel they need to be assertive and create an assertiveness statement they could use in that situation.

MINI LESSON STEPS:

1. The teacher should share the Assertive Speaking Template with students: "When I see (insert the situation), I feel (insert feeling) because (insert reason for the feeling). Would you be willing to (insert request)?" This can be shared by writing it on the board, using an online platform, posting a chart paper, or making copies to give to the class.

2. Next, the teacher can provide students with multiple scenarios that are age appropriate and

have students create assertive statements using the template. For example, ask students to come up with a statement they could say if they got an assignment back and were not happy with their mark. A possible statement could be, "When I see (I didn't get the mark I was hoping for on my assignment) I feel (frustrated) because (I worked really hard). Would you be willing to (explain my mark to me in more detail?)"

3. Students can share their statements and discuss them in a way the teacher feels fits the individual class, such as: self-reflection, a journal response, a whole-class discussion, a think-pair-share activity, or an online post or discussion.

4. Moving on, the teacher should ask students to think of a time in the past when they were not able to be assertive but wishes they had been. Using the template, students can create an assertiveness statement they could have used at that time in that situation. These statements could be shared in a way the teacher feels fits the class by using one of the methods mentioned above in Step 3.

5. Finally, students can think of a current situation where they feel they need to be more assertive and come up with their own assertiveness statement using the template. Again, students can share statements in a way the teacher sees fits the class as outlined in Step 3.

LESSON 3:
HOW TO SAY NO

Rationale: The ability to say no in an appropriate way is something that many students struggle with. However, the ability to say no is key to students feeling seen and heard and that what they say matters. Again, these skills can aid in self-advocacy and prevent extra stress and anxiety because too much has been taken on. Learning to say no in an appropriate way can also keep students safe if they find themselves in a situation where they are made to feel uncomfortable or as though their boundaries are being crossed.

LEARNING OUTCOMES

After this lesson students will be able to do the following:

- Understand the importance of saying no to others.

- Use the "Saying No" template to create statements to say no based on age-appropriate scenarios.

- Reflect on a time in their past when they wanted to say no but didn't, and create their own saying-no statement based on that past situation.

- Think of a current experience where they are having trouble saying no and create their own saying-no statement based on that situation. Students can then be given the option to share their statements in a way they feel comfortable.

MINI-LESSON STEPS

The teacher can lead a brainstorm activity with students on why it is sometimes challenging to say no to someone and discuss ideas as a class. Why is it hard to say no? Whom is it hard to say no to and why?

Building on the initial brainstorm activity, the teacher can lead another brainstorm, asking the class why it is important to say no sometimes, even though it can be challenging.

Next, the teacher can share the saying-no template with students: "I know that you want me to (insert the person's request), but I'm going to have to say no this time because (insert reason why you are saying no). Thank you for thinking of me."

The teacher can then provide students with multiple examples that are age appropriate, and have students create saying-no statements using the template. For example, ask students to use the template to come up with a statement to use if they were asked to volunteer for a school event that they didn't want to volunteer for. One possible statement could be, "I know you want me to volunteer for sports day, but I'm going to have to say no this time because I feel very busy right now with other commitments. Thank you for thinking of me."

Students can share and discuss their statements in a way the teacher feels are appropriate for the class.

Next, the teacher can ask students to think of a time in the past when they wanted to say no but didn't. Using the template, students can create their own saying-no statements that they could have used at the time in that situation. These statements could be shared in a way the teacher feels fits the class.

Finally, students can think of a current situation where they would like to say no but are having difficulty and create their own saying-no statement that they could use in that situation. Students can have the option to share their statements.

INCLUDING GARDNER'S MULTIPLE INTELLIGENCES IN THE LESSONS

Below are some ideas on ways to incorporate the Multiple Intelligence theory into the lessons I have shared. Teachers can select ones that are age- and subject area–appropriate based on the individual class.

- Visual/Spatial: Students can draw or use art to reflect one of the key concepts in the lessons. They can create a presentation on one of concepts, create a mind map or other type of chart or graph using one of the concepts, role play one of the concepts, or visualize ways to express the concept learned in class.

- Linguistic: Students can use their voices to tell a story about one of the concepts learned. They can take part in a word game, such as brainstorming on one of the concepts; take part in a discussion, write in a journal, or record themselves speaking on one of the concepts in the lessons.

- Logical/Mathematical: Students can problem solve, think critically, and use logic to explain and reflect on one of the lesson concepts.

- Body/Kinesthetic: Students can use drama or dance to express one of the concepts learned, use tactile art materials, or build something to demonstrate one of the concepts.

- Musical: Students can use instruments, recorded music, or create their own music to express, share, and reflect on one of the concepts learned in class.

- Interpersonal: Students can teach others about one of the concepts taught. They can be asked to cooperate with others in the classroom to reflect on or express one of the concepts in the lessons.

- Intrapersonal: Students can be asked to use a journal or do another form of self-reflection to think about one of the concepts in the lessons.

- Naturalistic: Students can reflect on how the concepts taught are seen in the natural world.

The skills of being assertive in the ways outlined above will empower students and help them to still feel seen and heard and that what they say matters outside of your classroom to another grade, post-secondary education, or the work force.

As the last part of the school year comes to a close, teachers should remember to thank students for being a part of the class and let them know you enjoyed teaching them and that you know they will be successful moving forward. After a year of making sure students feel seen and heard and that what they say matters I always end my classes this way. There have even been times when I wrote a personal note to each one of my students to take with them when they leave. Yes, this sometimes means that I have written up to ninety cards! It takes time but it is always worth it and is a final way to validate the student's role in the class.

TEACHER CHECKLIST

☐ Do you have the definitions of the words: passive, assertive, and aggressive ready to explain and discuss with students?

☐ Do you have the Assertiveness Speaking Template ready to share with the class?

☐ Do you have the Saying No template ready to share with the class?

☐ Have you set aside days to teach each of the lessons with the appropriate amount of time for each one based on the outline in this book?

☐ Have you thought of a way to thank students for being a part of the class verbally, in writing, or another way that expresses gratitude?

TEACHER AFFIRMATIONS

Pastor Joel Osteen speaks about the power of the "I am" statement in his sermon entitled, "The Power of I Am." He declares that "what follows these two words will determine what kind of life you live." He also states, "be careful what follows the 'I am' because you will receive it."[11]

As teachers, rarely do we get affirmed for our work by others. Students, parents, administration, and school boards don't often express how much they appreciate the work teachers do every day. Feeling seen and heard and that what we say matters is important not only for our students but for teachers as well.

Practising personal affirmations before and after the school day is a way for teachers to foster our own self-esteem and recognize ourselves for the work we do in our classrooms every day. Alternatively, teachers can affirm their colleagues in the same way, making sure that those we work with also feel seen and heard and that what they say matters.

Here are some affirmations that teachers can use to start and end the day, and I encourage readers to also come up with their own affirmations.

- I am becoming a better teacher every day.

- I am allowing my students to feel seen and heard and that what they say matters.

- I am prepared and ready for the day.

- I am making a difference in my students' lives.

- I am a valuable asset to the school where I teach.

- I am creating a safe space in my classroom for students to succeed.

- I am doing important work in my classroom.

- I am learning from my students every day.

- I am bringing positive energy to my classroom.

- I am doing the best I can with what I have been given at this time.

AFTERWORD

My hopes in writing this book are many. One is for other teachers to become aware of concrete ways they can use in their classrooms to make students feel seen and heard and that what they say matters. By putting these techniques into practice in classrooms, teachers can support students' safety and mental health. This can be life changing for students, especially those in the Black, Indigenous, LGBTQ+, special needs, and newcomers to Canadian communities.

Another hope in the writing of this book is for students to feel safe and for their mental health to be supported in as many classrooms as possible. So much of a young person's life is spent in a classroom with teachers. If students can leave the education system feeling seen and heard and that what they say matters they will be much more successful in their educational journey and after they leave.

I also hope that school boards and teacher-training institutions will read and learn from my book. If school boards and teacher-training programs train their staff and new teachers entering the profession on the techniques outlined in this book, a more wide-reaching effect will be felt by students everywhere in the country. A whole school board can become a place where students feel seen and heard and that what they say matters. Further, teacher-training programs can have graduating classes prepared to create a safe space in their classrooms that support students' mental health.

I developed these techniques over a number of years, seeing what worked and what I could improve on. I have engaged in discussions with my students and readily accepted any feedback they had for me on how they felt in my classroom. I have used all the techniques outlined in this book in my own classroom with much success. I know that they work for me and I am confident that they will work for others as well.

When I have a student tell me they feel safe in my classroom, have gained confidence in their abilities, and feel validated as a person, I am reminded of why I became a teacher. It was not so much to teach the curriculum, but instead to make a difference in the lives of young people. Even if just one student feels seen and heard and that what they say matters in the brief time I have the opportunity to teach them, it is worth the effort of creating a safe classroom environment where personal and academic learning can take place. Thank you for reading.

ENDNOTES

1. Carolyn Côté-Lussier and Caroline Fitzpatrick, "Feelings of Safety at School, Socioemotional Functioning, and Classroom Engagement," *Journal of Adolescent Health* 58, no. 5 (May 1, 2016): https://www.jahonline.org/article/S1054-139X(16)00020-3/fulltext.

2. Katherine Tombeau Cost, Jennifer Crosbie, Evdokia Anagnostou, et al., "Mostly Worse, Occasionally Better: Impact of COVID-19 Pandemic on the Mental Health of Canadian Children and Adolescents," *European Child & Adolescent Psychiatry*, February 26, 2021, accessed October 10, 2021, https://link.springer.com/article/10.1007%2Fs00787-021-01744-3.

3. Marie Kondo, "Brené Brown on How Gratitude Begets Joy," n.d., accessed October 10, 2021, https://konmari.com/brene-brown-interview/.

4. Marilynn K. Clayton, "Responsive Classroom: Displaying Student Work," August 18, 2010, accessed October 10, 2021, https://www.responsiveclassroom.org/displaying-student-work/.

5. Alexandra D. Owens, "Encouraging Students to Ask Questions," June 7, 2016, accessed October 10, 2021, https://edu.stemjobs.com/encouraging-students-to-ask-questions/.

6. Jeremy Dean, "Why 'Thank You' Is More Important Than Just Good Manners," September 15, 2010, accessed October 10, 2021, https://psychcentral.com/blog/why-thank-you-is-more-than-just-good-manners#1.

7. Dr. Kenneth Shore, "Encouraging Class Participation," n.d., accessed October 10, 2021, https://www.educationworld.com/a_curr/shore/shore056.shtml.

8. Chip Wood and Babs Freeman-Lotis, "Want Positive Behavior? Use Positive Language," April 10, 2012, accessed October 10, 2021, https://www.responsiveclassroom.org/want-positive-behavior-use-positive-language/.

9. Government of Ontario, "Human Rights, Equity, and Inclusive Education," n.d., accessed October 10, 2021, https://www. dcp.edu.gov.on.ca/en/program-planning/ considerations-for-program-planning/ human-rights-equity-and-inclusive-education.

10. School Mental Health Ontario (SMHO), "Educators Matter for Student Mental Health," n.d., accessed October 10, 2021, https://sm-ho-smso.ca/educators/your-role/.

11. Pastor Joel Osteen, "The Power of 'I AM.' What Follows the 'I AM' Is What You Will Become," July 31, 2015, accessed October 10, 2021, YouTube video: https://www.youtube.com/ watch?v=ueOdyBjqa1M.

ABOUT THE AUTHOR

 Kim Alexander was born in Thunder Bay, Ontario, and moved to Mississauga with her family when she was a young girl. After graduating high school, she attended the University of Toronto and completed her Honours Bachelor of Arts, majoring in English and History with a minor in Women's Studies. After attending the Ontario Institute of Educational Studies (OISE) and receiving her Bachelor of Education, Kim began her high school teaching career in 1999.

For her innovative work with Literature Circles in the classroom, Kim received the Ontario English Catholic Teachers' Association (OECTA) Best Practice Award in 2002. Noticing a mental-health crisis beginning in schools with little support for students, Kim returned to being a student herself, and in 2018 she completed her Certificate of Concurrent Disorders through the Centre for Addiction and Mental Health (CAMH) and the University of Toronto School of Medicine. Soon after she started a mental health–related course at the high school where she teaches, which runs with much success to this day.

When not teaching, Kim can be found reading everything from mysteries to biographies, practising power yoga, watching her beloved Toronto Maple Leafs, or taking long walks in the outdoors. She can be found on Twitter at @KimAlexander_.

CPSIA information can be obtained
at www.ICGtesting.com
Printed in the USA
BVHW060935271221
624881BV00002B/185